Grief
Road

Poems of Loss & Celebration

Vanessa Furse
Jackson

IRON
PRESS

First published 2019 by IRON Press
5 Marden Terrace
Cullercoats
North Shields
NE30 4PD
tel +44(0)191 2531901
ironpress@xlnmail.com
www.ironpress.co.uk

FIRST EDITION

ISBN 978 1-9997636-6-4
Printed by Imprint Digital

Cover and book design, Brian Grogan and Peter Mortimer

Typeset in Georgia 9pt
Titles Roboto Condensed Light 18pt
Cover Photograph by Miranda Johnson

IRON Press books are distributed by
NBN International
and represented by Inpress Ltd
Milburn House, Dean Street
Newcastle upon Tyne NE1 1LF
tel: +44(0)191 2308104
www.inpressbooks.co.uk

Supported using public funding by
ARTS COUNCIL ENGLAND
LOTTERY FUNDED

VANESSA FURSE JACKSON comes from a family with deep roots in Devonshire. However, married to Robb Jackson, an Ohio native, she lived in the United States for almost thirty years, the majority of them spent teaching literature and writing at Texas A&M University-Corpus Christi.

A book about her great-grandfather, *The Poetry of Henry Newbolt: Patriotism Is Not Enough*, was published in 1994 by ELT Press. Her first collection of short stories, *What I Cannot Say to You*, came out from the University of Missouri Press in 2003. Her second collection, *Small Displacements*, was published by Livingston Press in 2010 and won the PEN Texas 2011 Southwest Award for Fiction. She also co-authored a book of poems with her husband Robb, entitled *Crane Creek, Two Voices*, which was published by Fithian Press in 2011. Her first novel, *The Revolving Year*, came out in the Autumn of 2013 from Barking Rain Press. A second novel about the same characters, *The Anthropologist's Daughter,* was released by Barking Rain in June 2015.

Vanessa returned to England in January 2014, following Robb's death. She now lives just outside Winchester in Hampshire, where she runs a local writing group and walks in the countryside with her dog Jax.

The Background

ROBB AND VANESSA MET AT A UNIVERSITY IN THE STATES IN 1984. He was from the shores of Lake Erie in Ohio, she from England. Six weeks after Vanessa stepped off the plane, they were living together. Two years later, they were married. Robb had four small children (whom he adored) from his first marriage. Vanessa was almost 4,000 miles from home and her close family. Their relationship might so easily not have succeeded. But it did. The marriage was an exceptionally happy one.

They moved to Corpus Christi, Texas, and both taught in the same university department for over 20 years. The children all came and did their degrees there. Life was good. They bought a cabin just outside Big Bend National Park in West Texas. And they regularly visited England, particularly North Devon, from where Vanessa's family comes. Then, in 2008, Robb was diagnosed with rheumatoid arthritis. The disease became markedly worse over the next four years. Early in 2013, he went into hospital for a heart operation. He died twelve days later. He was sixty.

This collection of poetry explores the road she has been on since Robb's death and celebrates their life together.

The Journey

Writing *Grief Road*

Despite having written for most of my life, for two years after my husband Robb died I wrote nothing at all. Then I went on a writing retreat, run by a good friend who had known Robb and was an expert at coaxing others to write. She coaxed out of me the poem that began my writing of this book (*After He Died*). When I came home, I began tentatively to experiment with exploring the road I was on. I started to keep a journal and to work with a journal therapist. But I discovered that it was through the medium of poetry that I could reach the deepest understanding of my journey of grief and how to deal with it.

From that first poem, I moved both backward and forward in time. I began to celebrate moments we'd shared together, our wedding, holidays, adventures, even happy times quite close to his death. That proved very cathartic. At the same time, I wrote about how I was feeling as I went about my daily life in the place to which I had moved: the Itchen Valley in Hampshire. I walked and watched and listened, trying to capture with honesty both my experiences and my reactions to these. Gradually, I began to realize I was writing a linked series of poems for and about Robb, poems that mourned his death but that also celebrated his life.

When writing a poem, I usually begin with a strong image in the mind, which then forms a line or phrase that excites me into discovering what happens next. Each poem must form itself into an intellectual and emotional journey, inextricably connected by the music in words. I draft and redraft, over and over again, at first on paper and then on the computer. I read the poem aloud. I listen to it. I fiddle around obsessively with lines and words. That's the craft that must follow the initial magical impetus. I love it. The whole process of writing a poem is supremely engrossing, and that, too, is cathartic.

Grief Road took me on a long and sometimes difficult journey. But it allowed me to explore, in a way I don't think anything else could have done, the effect of loss and the possibility of renewal.

Vanessa Furse Jackson

For Leah, Ben, Josh and Luke

Listening to the Radio Tonight

Rain splattering the roof,
I've settled into a solitary rhythm,
resisting the recognition
that I could be doing this full time
should you die first.

What would I do
with all these spare moments?

I fend this thought off,
knowing you'll be home
in a couple of weeks,
that I can reach you by phone
though you're a quarter-of-the-earth
away from me now.

There's a day coming
when we won't be
together like we are,
sure as winter rain,

when one of us goes
beyond the pall to that place
only love can breach.

Robb Jackson
January 2011

Wedding

"May God add His blessing and keep you
to fulfill your covenant from this day forth,"
the judge said. He shook our hands
and there it was. We were married.
We left his solemn office, silent, dazed,
and went across the road to McDonald's
where we ordered two quarter-pounders
with fries to go. I laid my left hand on
the counter, the silver around my finger
glitteringly new. I wanted everyone there
to see and feel as amazed as I, as shining.
In our overloaded Datsun, we headed south
for Portsmouth, Ohio. Geese veed the sky
under the low November sun, and the road
flashed golden past us. We switched on
our chosen music—Purcell's *Glad Tidings*
with that impossible bass, from whose depths
the trebles burst up into sudden glorious joy.
We stole glances and smiles, beginning to believe
as we listened, dipping our fries in ketchup.

Leavings

Driftwood in the hand and in the heart,
picked up along the shores of Lake Erie, his home,
though back then both of us were learning a new
found land, love and the hurt that tugs beneath its surface—
explanations to his children that drenched our world in grief
and guilt, while at same time astonishing and exalting us
with the enormity of the gift we'd been granted.
Love again, always it came back to love and to pain,
to egrets and cormorants, bald eagles, chains of fox prints
in the snow, the bee tree's honey-dark hole, raccoons
curled sleeping in a hickory fork. Along the sickle
of the curving lakeshore, we wandered hand in hand,
looking for poems, stooping for shells and water-licked
driftwood—a small piece, warm, to fit into the palm
like a cross, a fossilized lizard twisted from root,
a deer-horn, a fish, an old man's face, an X for a kiss.

We pocketed tokens, talismans seemingly sent at random
yet meant for us only, promises, we said, to be kept.
Sometimes we tramped half a mile with a bone-white
rippled plank, massive as lead but lithe with possibility,
or a wind-scarred limb of timber we knew was right, ready
to slide into place, our place. First a sturdy bookshelf from found
wood furrowed with travelling, then a stocky table, fantastically
gnarled. I have it still, brought back to the old country, a piece
of flotsam that has reached the shore where he no longer lives.
Memories stack up in the sands of time, stripped bare of skin and bark
and him held drifting in the hand and in the heart.

Wish Fulfillment

I imagined you so often when I was on my own and lonely.
Not you exactly, you understand (how could I?),
but a kind of you, a vision, a you who would become me
when we'd found each other and conjoined our lives.

It was a fantasy, of course, a wish, a fairy tale I was careful
not to believe—of the youngest son, the knight, the prince
on a white horse whose coming would transform my life
from single into something both magical and simple.

Such wishes evade an easy granting. After all, life is
neither that magical nor that simple. We knew this, yet
we welcomed the charmed spell. Meeting in a foreign country
we claimed it for our own—our home. There was no more

imagining, no close examination of what we'd been given,
just a fearful rapture that at the journey's end was this beginning.
We didn't foresee the pain we would in fact cause, would feel,
would ultimately understand comes integral to the gift.

Joy and sorrow, that ecstatic, melancholic mingling, beloved
of poets, was the dragon we discovered we had not to slay,
nor even to overcome, but to accept as part of the bargain,
a compromise even as we promised in sickness and in health.

Your children are their own successes now. You'd be proud
of the ways they've grown, what they've learned about love
and truth. But within them, each must carry the bereft child
whose father left them long ago—and then again in death.

There are no words to comfort. Yes, you were my fantasy
made actual, the all I had envisioned, though you'd laugh, I know,
at the thought of yourself on any horse or dressed in princely guise.
Were we right, though, to accept the gift? Am I wrong to question it?

Reluctantly, I guess the answers lie in the foreign land that, childlike,
we wandered into, only half grasping the strange new language
we stammered at one another. Traduced, enchanted, gilded
by love, we buried scruple, falling headlong and terrified from grace.

The Lark Ascending

How, at the end, that lone violin catches
flight, song rising beyond comprehension
till it slips through silence in a thread of blue.

I was pathless in the dark forest when we met,
a stranger stumbling a new country, voiceless
among wild birds crying incoherently.

You gave me such gifts. Mind, hearing, sight
illumined. Thousands of geese rose as one for us,
goldfinches swirled in the milkweed, trilling,

and I understood. I opened my palm, life-lines
to a smaller land where sea and sky become one
and the cliff grass, green, hides singers in it

that spring up as if fired from under the ground,
quick in a spiralling glory of voice, the poets,
the skylarks who soar so enviably close to God.

Back and forth from your land to mine we flew,
both of us carrying the other's life as our own
in joy, as if the ascending music had no end.

How, alone now, I stand on the green cliffs,
where the larks still lift into infinite threads
of blue. And it is your song I am listening to.

Afterwords

I never told you that above the pall of cloud
the sky was blue because, of course, you knew
that every night the star field sang aloud
and the moon wandered on to another place,
shape-shifting across space.

Walking the quiet of the Chihuahuan Desert
where hummingbird wings startle the still air
or glorying in the gull-shrill cliffs of Devon
I don't remember talking about being there.
It was enough just to share.

I never spoke to you of beech unfurling spring
leaf by leaf. It didn't seem necessary
to put into words the silence of snow falling
or the river's voice purling to its estuary
and the marsh birds calling.

Halsdon Mill Cottage
(North Devon)

I.

One early evening, after
a long journey to this cottage
at the bottom of the woods,
I was upstairs making the bed,
breathing in the creamy quiet
of that lovely room beneath the thatch,
when through a closed window
a pheasant smashed in like a bomb,
scattering glass that had once
been engraved with a poem
from a husband to his young wife,
a keepsake when he went to war.

You collected the stunned bird
in a towel, took it downstairs,
and let it go in the garden, groggy.
I collected the shards of glass
with a dustpan and brush
and poured them away, one
lost word at a time.

II.

Gold flickers in the eye
of a late May morning.
You are writing a poem
in the other room, so I
get up from the kitchen table
and walk out
into the honeyed green
of a garden slipping into wild.
The stream sparkles over
its round grey stones, while
on the high field opposite
black and white cows
doze the soft air. Somewhere
a chiff-chaff whistles up Heaven
again and again.
A surge of happiness
washes through my body,
clean and dazzling as shock.

III.
Grey scarves
of mizzle
were drifting by
thatch dripping.

Standing
at the window
we spotted a deer
picking her way

delicately
upstream.
We saw her as though
through gauze.

IV

Alders lean over the rolling water, dipping leaf tips
into their own reflection to make arches of liquid shadow
along the river's lazy curve. The air hangs still and sleepy.

We're lying back untidily on the sheep-scented bank,
replete with wine and pasties, soporific, barefoot,
bedded in the quiet valley's palm, the sun's benison, when

from the dark gold of a low-slung branch a kingfisher
zips an iridescent streak across our eyes so fast we only
half see it before it arrows back downriver to shoot the bend.

We stand unsteadily, hands shading our eyes; we creep over
the warm stones to the water's edge, unwilling to believe
in such a brilliant vanishing. Our feet in the shallows are dim as fish.

Later, walking home, we disturb the guardian of the valley,
the grey heron who rises silently on monumental wings
and sails calm currents into the harbour at wood's edge.

Up through cloudy oaks and the clatter of pigeons, we climb,
lit by the kingfisher's quick blue blur, the heron's elegant ghost,
visions to save for a winter's night in some country far away.

V.

You talked often of those times at the cottage
when we walked up the lanes to the village to visit
the butcher for a small leg of lamb, the general store
for cream and other indulgences, and the graveyard
for communion with the dead.

All seemed so connected there in the church's breath
of quiet green—easy, almost. We live and then we die.
Over the years, the carved italics sink back into
the grey stones, and grief seems alien to the blackbird
singing from the ivied wall.

You liked to stand by the twisted yew, beneath which
my grandparents lay beside their eldest daughter,
the young wife who died too soon, not long after
her husband had engraved on their bedroom window
a poem to remind her of his love.

Morwenstow
(Cornwall)

Do you remember the long-eared owl of a church,
hunched down beside its combe above the wrecking
granite coast? In the graveyard, under rook-high trees,
stood the carved white figurehead of the good ship *Caledonia*,
crew and cargo smashed against Sharpnose Point in 1843.

And do you remember walking through those two small fields,
sheep grazing in mist, half-seen in the quiet crunch of grass,
from the furled church down to the astonishing roar beyond
the cliff's lip, sudden breath-sucked void, the sea hurling itself
repeatedly at rock-grey ribbons, the dragon-teeth of shore?

If you do, then you'll remember also the way I clung to you
at the gale of edge, compelled to lean out too far, terrified
of flying, of plunging past the ravens and the gulls below
to plummet deep beneath the rocks.
                                        It's all still there,
church, mist, sheep, cliffs. In my mind it drifts eternally,
a peripheral vision just out of sight, sea-loud, insistent,
calling me when the day is dark to lean, lean over, fly at last—
—and you no longer here.

Embury Beacon

(Devon)

We sit five hundred feet above the sea
and the sun always shines on us here.
We are alone. We are together.
Every year the air is golden with
the coconut scent of gorse,
and the coastline reels away from us
in giddy casts to north and south.
The grass is prickly and sweet, starred
with thrift and sheep's-bit, clover, heather,
foxgloves spear-straight in the hollows.

We're in an iron-age promontory fort
or what is left after the hungry incursions
of tides, three thousand years of history
sensed only by the outline of its absence.

Larks sing invisibly above us
while below the cliff edge, ravens
fly then flip to glide past upside down.
The sea's skin stretches out supple
towards the horizon's brim, down which
it falls from sight. We shut our eyes,
lulled by cider and serenity,
wholly held in this bowl of time, this now,
this seemingly forever afternoon.

I shan't return. The Beacon will tend
its past as it has always done, eroding
memory year by infinitesimal year,
warm in the aromatic summer sun.
It will welcome other lovers there, others
to defend that which is held most dear.

Departure

For seven hours I sat in the Heathrow terminal, watching
the snow fall—flight delayed then announced then delayed—
and though I sat without moving, I was filled with a storm
of despair that swelled and raged within me because I couldn't
get home to him. Still the snow fell beyond the window,
silently insistent. Feeling my muscles clench to iron, I thought
this is grief—this is what an ocean of absence would feel like,
this raging, this blizzard, the willful departure from all that my heart
most craves, this railing against God or fate or implacable crystals
of ice.

      I was wrong, of course. For grief is not the interminable wait at
the airport for a plane that takes off seven hours late, nosing up through
the sullen belly of clouds to a sun that was patiently waiting there all the
time. It is not the flight towards him at the gate, his familiar awkward
hug, the tired drive home to the weaving, purring cats.
What was I thinking that day in the terminal?
What was the snow saying?

Texas Farm Road after Late Summer Rain

The road has been washed down to bone
white caliche between its pulsing gullies, arteries
of muddy water lit by scarlet dragonflies,
bright biplanes hovering over clouds of rain lilies
waiting for the million new mosquitoes born of storms.

On pole after pole above the rich and stinking ditches
caracaras sit with carrion eye, hawks crouch, harsh feet
held taut, intent, content to wait the easy swoop for
mouse or squirrel, horny toad or lizard running carelessly
from weeks of drought to wet fecundity, the gift of rain.

We list each sighting, grateful, soothed, surprised
again at such abundance sprung from out this thirsty
worn, dirt-poor South Texas land, like calico lantana
flashing its pennies of sun at the mockingbird who gulps
its berry clusters as he calls in his best dove voice.

Wings held out like the arms of unsteady children,
roadrunners (overgrown cuckoos) on sprung feet leap
across our path, find camouflage on low branches
of mesquite, dappled dark and hung with incongruous
mistletoe. We laugh, sigh at the road's end,

grip hands together and send an ardent prayer
that such generative rain will always bring green
after drought and hope after sorrow, will spring
miraculous from the rock of the dry and unforgiving
desert to bloom as bright as peace in the sand.

On the way home a sweep of low brush
is flowered with egrets fishing the fields
where Petronila Creek has slipped its banks
and is quietly silvering the land.

A Tale from Mesa Verde

(Colorado)

We were walking by the cliff dwellings
of the Anasazi. The air was spiced with resin,
the canyon drowsy in the heat. Chipmunks
chattered drily in a nearby juniper bush;
otherwise all was still and fragrant, hot—
an afternoon in trance. Suddenly a crow
stumbled hurt from the fir and piñon pine
onto the path in front of us. Shocked,
as if out of a dream, we stood to watch.
A gray jay, shouting from a chokecherry,
flung up an echo that swerved around
high rock, sounding again and again.
The crow tilted her head as if to check
we were really paying attention.
I'm hurt, I'm very hurt!
The jay mocked as Crow dragged
her wounded wing in the piney dust,
limping sadly along before us.
Surely the sun was too benign,
too golden to countenance such death?
We followed behind, half reluctantly,
helpless. High above the fragrant pines
two vultures swung lazily, waiting
with us. We crept around a bitterbrush,
hearts beating fast. Stopped. Exactly then,
in one explosive thrust, the victim blasted up
and with a harsh cry of victory, vanished.
We were the fools, she the jubilant saviour
of her hidden nest. The clicking chatter
of chipmunks sounded now like laughter.
One day, Crow, we said, one fine day
you will cry *Wolf*, and out of the trees
he'll come trotting past your trickery
to head straight for the tender chicks.
And that will be another tale.

Christmas in the Chihuahuan Desert
(Big Bend National Park, West Texas)

We owned a small adobe cabin at Lajitas, nothing special
I suppose, but there we made a sanctuary from harm. Outside
the dazzling ribbon of the Rio Grande slipped blue through
thrusting canyons, high as thunderheads, while in the distance
a slick of snow lit up the peaks of the Chisos Mountains.

Everything flickers on, scenes fixed in the insistent repository
of mind—not pictures of nostalgia but, as it were, of now. Still
those thick green globes of mistletoe in the mesquite scrub,
the quick scarlet flight of cardinals, the desert willow's pink
and delicate blooms buzzing with ruby-throated hummingbirds.

Still night in the icy sky, brilliant garlands of dizzying stars
that carolled down the thin black air, swooping, blinding, till
we'd lose our balance and have to stumble back into the cabin.
Here were candles and a crackling fire to veil the shadows
of a New Year crouched just out of sight, concealing its surprise.

Mule Ears Peak
(Big Bend)

Grateful for the sun's warming in the stiffness of winter
we sit on low stones between honey mesquite and creosote,
resting after the difficult balance of a narrow trail clinkered
with lava, made dangerous by the distraction of beauty.

Listening to the dense stillness of desert silence, we hear
the clatter of a bird's wings behind us as footsteps
approaching. For a quickened moment, our hearts beat fast
as if to warn us we're not alone in our sanctuary after all—

as if something restless had shadowed us here, had come
to stand at our shoulders, one hand raised to shade its eyes,
to bid us gaze on the stone-spired ears that in the crafty light
have become cathedral towers thronged with spirits surely

praising the golden slant of this one minute, choired in vision only.
We blink and breathe. No bird is visible when we rise to leave. Silently
we carry the fragile shell of vision home, watching with wakeful care
our clumsy wingless feet on the shifting ground beneath us.

Last Anniversary
(Big Bend)

I'm sitting on the cool grey slabs
of stone by Cattail Falls, watching
scarlet dragonflies flit the ferns
and yellow butterflies wing petals
beneath oaks. Beyond me, you're climbing
tumbled sprawls of rock, your boots slipping
small chips into crevices, my heart
into my mouth.

I want to say, "Come back where you
are safe, don't risk a fall, take care!"
But fear is dangerous, and love cannot
keep safe the heart by building it
a cage. So I pray silently

lifting my eyes from the shadows
to the lion-skinned cliffs that spring
sheer upward from the sheltered falls
into the fierce uncompromising heat
above.
          I ask that greater love will
keep us safe, will grant the gift of time,
return us here again to balance on
precarious stones, to listen as
the canyon wren's hymned echoes
slip between high walls to bless us.
May we hold this day forever.

On Reflection

Neither of us broke a mirror before it happened.
There was no signalled intimation of mortality.
Had there been such a shattering, I'd have taken
the frame and shards of glass and buried them
deep in the earth beneath a pale new moon.

I would have placated any god for you, any lingering
superstition, walked around ladders, thrown spilt salt
over my left shoulder, saluted all single magpies.
I would have bargained with Mephistopheles.
Well, of course I would.

Afterwards, I didn't cover up the mirrors in the house
or turn them to the wall, as people will who believe
the departing spirit can get trapped in the glass
as it struggles back to possess the living.

There was no point. I am anyway possessed
by your absence and its spectral twin, your presence,
locked in me, poor prisoners.

When I catch sight of myself in a mirror now, I see a face
I recognise only slightly, caught in reluctant reflection,
someone older whom I might one day become,
long after you are gone.

Hospital

Outside the high window
the unconfined world went
silently about its business,
gulls and pelicans dipping
white wings over
the gold-scalloped water
of Corpus Christi Bay,
the city streaming by,
each life intent, intentioned.

We were in a safe place then,
a room suffused with light
and (I can say this now)
a calm and particular strain
of innocence. We were
as if in some far tower,
thick-walled, protected,
everything but the moment
fallen away.

We spent the waiting
lightly, laughing together,
held in a sunlit buoyancy
that gentled us
above the plunging
gravity of fear.

So when I look back
to the surgery, I see you
not as you were afterwards,
your body jumping, outraged
with pain, your self lost
in the dusky torpor
of intensive care,
but as you were
in my care, lit
with the morning's grace,
and happy perhaps
for the last time.

After He Died

No-one asked me if I was all right.
They said, wait over there by that window,
and when you see a green taxi pull up
it will be for you. They wanted me gone
because a hospital's early morning shift
does not like to begin with bereavement.

The driver smelled of sweat and cigarettes
and talked about how life had never
given him a chance. At the kerb
where he dropped me, a large black glove
lay in the road, lost, I suppose,
by one of the paramedics in the dark.
I unlocked the front door and walked into a house
whose life support had just been switched off.

Stone

In the end I chose to have
Love is stronger than death
engraved on his headstone.

But the granite slab seems
stronger still, sometimes
making it hard to breathe.

Beneath the weight, his heart
is inert ash, while mine is
walled in fire and stone.

For Which There Are No Answers

And sometimes I think as I stare through the window
at unblinking blue above a thrust of cloud
that he's out there somewhere just beyond—
that he must be because the box of ash
we buried in the earth beneath a rook-tossed sky
in an Ohio cornfield was merely the remains
of the body, the part he anyway disliked,
shambolic animal become mortal enemy.

I wonder if we who are left all ask
the same questions after death: where
do the parts we cannot bury go, the soul,
the unnamable essence, indivisible love?
Is memory the return of spirit? If it is,
why does it comfort with so sharp a sting?
As I watch the clouds mass, I think that once
he and I would have sat and talked about this.

Prayer

In the mouth
anger turns
bitter as the milk
of dandelions.
It shudders
on the tongue,
impossible
to swallow.

Dear God,
let me not
seek nourishment
in the roots
of despair.
Entrust to me
sweet apples,
honeysuckle
and the singing
of bees
in the endless
days to come.

You Ask Me How I Feel

It's hard to tell. But as if I can't help
clutching at jagged pieces of wood,
at a broken box of photographs,
or inadvertently catching myself
on barbed regret, until my skin
is shot with splinters that can only
be tweezered out with painstaking
persistence.

Or I'm walking a green bridleway
in the southern English spring,
when through the soft leaves
a prickly pear claws quick at me,
drawing blood, and I'm cast back
onto a familiar desert floor,
picking at spines so tiny I feel pain
I cannot see.

As if this unexpected journey of grief
demands as fee a constant plucking,
pulling out sharp stings of memory
again and again.

Turning

A morning tentative with mist:
the small flock of sheep
must dip their heads into
the meadow's breath
to scent the grass beneath.

Stern reaches of upper sky
have slipped past yesterday's
green warmth to touch
the tips of beech and ash
with intimations of rust.

All day long swifts tumble
the high cloud, throwing
themselves at the wind
as if seeking directions
for the journey south.

Tomorrow, I understand,
summer will have flown.
Everything travels
further away from death,
yet always towards it again.

Thanksgiving

People grumble about the way winter
steals time, the way it grows bolder
each day, as if we might not notice
it draining the afternoons of colour,
pulling blinds down over the ragged sky.

I like them, though, those long dark evenings
that shut out thought and the need to act.
I turn up the heat and wait at the window
as the air greys and swans gather together
on the river beyond fading water meadows.

Grateful not to be reminded of spring light
and the cyclical hurts that accompany rebirth,
I watch the bare trees blur, become lost,
till all I can see in the panes of black glass
is my own reflection, transient as snow.

Winter Solstice

Day after day
this grey December,
I've malingered
in a whorl of shell
or drifted
while the fragile mist
of dimming afternoons
grows still and cold.

Suspended,
neither mourning
nor remembering,
I watch the world
through glass:

swans on the river,
the fox at dusk,
his tawny shadow
floating over
insubstantial grass,
the last gulls
sleeping down the sky,
all quiet, mute.

Only the stealthy rise
of the round moon
quickens the pulse.
Its pure, divining eye
transfixes, seeks out
denials, secrets,
shining a silver light
on the small chip of ice
in the heart.

New Year

In the dead of winter
the quickening of spring
lies dormant. How easily
come the words, how hard
their unpitched resonance.
The dead do not lie
dormant. They aren't as if
in sleep—they do not dream
nor will they quicken.
The dead do not lie to rise

as sap, to swell as tender
buds. The dead are become
ash, burned out and spread
on earth, or stones buried
under ground forever
fallow, never to be blessed
by the concept of spring.

Yet the living, even in grief,
believe, if grudgingly,
in words that resonate,
in the promised coming
of a green season, even,
sometimes, in poetry.

In the depths of sorrow
is there possibility?
A shift in the wind, a hint
of light that seems a shade
less dull than yesterday?
Tell all the truth but tell it slant,
the poet says. Be gentle then.
What lies so dormant? What is it
insisting in the dead of winter
that the tough business of living
may be vital after all?

Giving Way

On a greying winter afternoon,
austere, stiff to the bone,
nothing moves. The landscape
has turned away its face.

What is beyond the window
is in the room also:
a paralysis of soul, a freeze,
this numb flinch from memories.

Solitude makes a sanctuary
but loneliness an absence
and a harm. Evening grips the skin,
lowers the blind. Lets the dark in.

Yew Hill, Compton Down
(Hampshire)

On a blue and bitter January morning
my eyes stream in the knifing wind
and the wide landscape fractures
into random shards of field and sky.

The sun tugs in vain at the taut strings
of these short days, struggling to offer light
brighter than straw. Except for the defiant
green of ivy, every shade seems dull or dying.

I think, as I stand on this high hill where
I've stood so often before, that we imprint
our lives over and over as if to perfect
a pattern that we never quite discern.

Below me, blackbirds toss and tumble through
the uncontrollable air. Last time I was here
it was summer and you were with me, butterflies
spreading their wings in the warm grass.

Through a High Window

This was a morning smoked with frost.
The sun was struggling to rise
into the thin blue sky, as if tethered
to an iron-ringed horizon.
Yet on the brittle tips of a solitary oak,
displayed like ornaments, perfectly still,
four egrets, white as snow and stroked
by the pale light, sat poised above
the chill river, heads turned to the water
that was towing winter down to the sea.

Surely there weren't white egrets here
when I was young? To see them now
is to suppose I might have wrapped them
safe with the other cherished things
I shipped back home from Texas, perhaps
to remind me of the life of water,
its commonality, its fluid encompassing
of past and present, of all who travel
across dissolving borders to another land.

I stood by the window as the sun broke free
and slanted its low gold across the meadow.
Memory burst its cage, beat wings against
the dusty attic glass, and either that soft
thrumming or a warmth on white feathers
woke the egrets into flight. I watched them
leave, drifting low-misted down the quiet
current out of sight.
                    Still I saw them, though,
standing in the shallows of Oso Bay, fishing by
the Gulf of Mexico, at home in the hot salt sun,
just as I remember them.

Psalm

I have been acquainted with the night, with grief.
But I'm acquainted with sorrow only because
I have known the grace of hills, the sunlit uplands,
lapwings, larks ascending beyond the infinite ecstasy
of blue. I have held the living warmth of my lover,
my friend. I have embraced the precarious certainty
of him, the premonition of loss—because there is nothing
in this world so precious as the dangerous joy of absolute
union. He wrote me poems. In one he said:

There's a day coming
when we won't be
together like we are,
sure as winter rain,

when one of us goes
beyond the pall to that place
only love can breach.

And he has gone. Yet I wouldn't exchange this pain
for the safe trudge of the lowlands. The larksong height
of passion is perhaps only fully comprehended
from the unforgiving depths of the dark river,
where the boatman takes his toll, I've discovered,
not from the dead but from the living. I pay not willingly
but with mute thanks for the terrible beauty of life.

And to Hold

You're standing in the living room by your chair
—getting ready to leave the house perhaps—
and I hug you, drawing you inward,
closing my eyes to absorb your familiar scent,
your body, the particular curve of your arms,
the essence of you who are partly me.

Even now I can do this, closing my eyes
and willing myself to go back to your country,
your comfort, the warmth of just standing still
together. Only the scent is fading, slowly,
as if a tenuous breeze were blowing
its elusive breath to fill some empty place.

Falling Awake

If I could fly tonight
like the white bird gold in low sun,
it would be to the oaks' height,
to the underside of spiry leaves.
They clutch at their gusting twigs
whose treacherous grasp conceals
summer's fall to come, not yet but always
before we're ready to let go.

The moon slips down
the silver river, helpless and thin,
on muscled eddies fighting each other
for a first feel of the tide. Shadows
shift uneasily beneath the egret's nest.
Foxes bark a warning; weasels
bite the screaming rabbits' necks,
as I cower warm in white sheets.

If I were braver, could uncurl,
I'd creep outside to shiver where,
in the metalled blue-black air,
I'd witness the poacher's loneliness
in the bloodied grass, the betrayal
of leaves, the moon's quiet slide
to a sea on the other side of the world.
I'd be there, not here awake
and fearful in this dreamless room.

Easter

And then, one morning, something green on the wing
tilts the wind just so. A fractional shift but warm.
The air hums. The swans on the river shine white
and lovely. Jays dip, flash, skim outside my window
and rabbit kits, fragile and fearless, romp in the grass.
Along the lane the banks are pricked with sun-stars,
golden celandines glittering upward. The wren flits by
like a mouse then, hidden, sings in the ash whose tight
black horseshoes are splitting open with the shimmer
of birthing leaves.
     All is rising, all things reaching
for the blue height, the resurrection coming, the new
season, and for a moment I believe I have the faith
to rise, too. Quick, the leaves say. Quick before doubt
pulls us back into the numbing grip of winter.

Letter in Spring

As the land greens and leaves unfurl
(although people are still unkind)
I want to love you in words again,
not spoken to a ghost or inked in
the certainty of print, but pencilled
in a shaky scrawl of overwhelming
need, fighting through the mind's
dense scribbles, its chaotic lines.

Winter swallows speech. Words lie
beneath the silent snow, the hard
drowning of ice. Despair is the easiest
silence. But now, new images claw
the page like lions on the March wind.
I have so much to tell you. It is spring,
vibrant with song, and yet I'm mute, facing
that time of year when absence is reborn.

May Day

Today is your birthday, and I want to give you something
special. I'm thinking of choosing the horse-chestnut trees
that have just lit their blossoming candles among soft explosions
of new leaves. Or perhaps the swans nudging their leggy cygnets
into the reeds where the warbler sings. You could have a scurry
of inland gulls shouting like children, or in the meadow sheep
gazing with stolid perplexity at their zany, bouncing lambs.
But maybe you'd like the swallows feather-stitching the sky,
the cuckoo fluting over copper beeches, trout hurling silver
bodies up in glittering showers from the river. The whole
valley is rich, singing and thick with abundance to be given.
What would you wish for this warm celebratory day?
                                        I wonder if you'd
choose the rain drifting slowly in from the west, the gift that will fall
to bless the leaves and gulls and reeds, and we
who shall all grow out of the dark earth. Today is your birthday,
but all I can find to give are words to comfort the living.

Walking the Itchen Navigation Way

Picture two wrens, one in song
on a blackthorn twig, the other
scampering like a field mouse
through the sweetgrass by the river;
purple loosestrife, comfrey, wild mint,
swifts lassoing bugs above red admirals
spread out like silk rugs on my path;
trout nosing circles on water's surface
where stars of crowfoot flowers float;
two swans, fierce-faced, with silver cygnets,
watching a spaniel shake a glitter of drops
around me, red kites circling up
on thermals above the valley, a white
egret stabbing at small fry in the shallows;
among a field of brown and white
Jacob's sheep, three emus graze,
occasionally lifting small placid heads
to gaze across the hedge at a meadow
full of llamas.
                    An unexpected walk,
I thought, a lifting up, if not to happiness,
then to something that could grow perhaps
next spring, could yet surprise with flower.

Echoes from a Dark Evening

After a day so long and hot,
so high and vaulted
it could have been a holiday,
I stood in the honeyed dark
and watched the bats—
a suddenness of skin wings
in the sky, blind-flying,
carefully fingering the night—
a conception of the universe
as merely a succession of sounds
returned to signal danger:
avoid this star, and this!

I wanted to turn and speak
but I stayed quiet, still.
I too am careful to avoid
headlong meetings or other
obstacles in my path.

Later, I slept in the summer night,
turned inward from the dark,
locked in tumbling dreams
of wild unsettling wings
and a wind that blew us
senseless and gasping
in random terror about the sky.

I woke to the oblivious light,
remembering with sorrow only
how urgently I wanted to turn
to you last night and say, *Look
how they swerve from danger,
how they fly between star
and star!*

Kestrels

Visiting your children, your country this summer
I met beauty and sorrow on a narrow path in the Blue
Mountains, where the air stung with pine and the fawns
were dappled and unafraid. Your absence walked
the same path. You should have been there.
Golden and purple lupins bloomed, violets, milkvetch,
Indian paintbrush and chipmunks who chased over rocks,
all entering the memory through new doors. It hurt
as of course it would. I've known your children for over
thirty years: their eyes so like yours, the hugs they must
have inherited. A hard visit, filled with gifts, kindness,
love that tugged at the parting, insistent, and came along
to the airport gates, grieving in silence on the plane.

Back home, the journey spooling through my mind's fatigue,
I was met by the fluting screels of three young kestrels,
recently fledged and taking for play space my roof terrace,
window sills, flower pots. Striplings who jostled, strutted,
peered in at me with gold-ringed eyes then scythed down
to the river, returning triumphant with a flattened mouse
to lay on my terrace table, as if offering a tangible reward
for learning to dive from such heights. So, gifts here, too,
and along the path I walk daily, traveller's joy, self-heal,
meadowsweet, honeysuckle, all things busy with summer,
the beauty and sorrow that thread the hedges, kestrels
flying their breathtaking trust away to the beginning of fall.

Coming Around

Last week the first geese sounded mournfully down
the valley toward the migrant sea, and in their place
the swans came back from the cygnet months
to grace the river with their beautiful disdain.

Berries clung in hedges, and tiny wild plums
remembered folk long gone from cottage gardens
once so sweet with harvest. The barley wind
had swept great golden combs of hills quite bare
and sighed into nostalgia for the loss of languid days.

In the air instead, a chill of bonfire hinted at a falling
of fevered leaves and snow slung ready in a lowered
net of bruised and yellow sky. Not yet, but still too soon
I sensed the cold to come, the dark, the scent of frost.

But now today,
                        first a greening rain before the breeze
shifts. And next, as if to mock my autumn melancholy,
from a phoenix south there rises such a siren sun
that folk must leave their homes for the beckoning sea,
where astonished children sport upon the shore, and all
is holiday and forgetting and the hot surprise of joy.

I should know by now—nothing is straightforward,
nothing linear in the journeying of time or love or grief.
Everything recurs; clouds coil and uncurl in the circling sky;
geese fly the curve of earth; the vanishing moon returns
to mourn again.

Changed Utterly

I can make
no sense of rain
this August day
dribbling inert
down the dusty
window pane
outside
the sun shone
for so long
through July
that I too easily
believed
in warmth
forever
as I did until
the doctor knelt
before me
saying
his brain is
damaged
we need
your agreement
to withdraw
support.

I touched
his icy hand
in the moment
of death
not months
but years ago
since when
nothing
to speak of
has made
much sense
not even
my consent.

Gone but Not

Last night I dreamed you were ill. You couldn't sleep.
Your face was drawn. You had to go abroad, you said,
or lose everything. So I helped you find the clothes
you needed, all the time feeling the frantic anguish
of fear—of hurry, hurry, or...

You left while I wasn't looking, so I ran after you
down a steep hill to the busy street where you were
wheeling your suitcase through dense crowds.
I almost stopped you, till you turned to look at me,
mutely pleading, and I had to let you go.

But when I woke you were already dead, had died
some years ago. How could I have forgotten, even
in the slumbering dark? What impress of urgency
lodges so deep within the psyche that it's able to be
born again into a dream on such a random night?

Since waking, I've been worrying that perhaps
you came to give me something that had slipped
my mind and now has gone forever. Tell me why
you couldn't sleep. Where did the busy street lead?
Am I meant to interpret, remember or forget?

October Storm

First, beech trees flush to an apple-skin red
as if ripening their leaves for death, then these
start raining autumn in flurried handfuls
across the road, where they stick like moth wings
to the windscreens of passing cars. Small clouds
hurry, running for home, bumping into each other
till their edges bruise, and they swell and thicken
in the heavy yellow sky.

I feel the wind as anger, thrusting its face too close
to mine. The rain chases leaves across the road
in whipping scurries, headlights swerve and blur
and I must bend my head against the thrusting
bullying air, must keep feet firmly planted, not give in.
If I were rabbit or fox, I'd have a den, not merely my own
thin skin, no match for the buffeting winds. I'd have
the warmth of a den-mate in the darkest times of storm.
I certainly wouldn't be standing at the side of the road
in this ridiculous despair.

Grief Road

I.

It's dark. The track is treacherous with footprints, littered
with pilgrims' complaints tacked up on wayside shrines,
damp, scribbled pleas to saints obscurely personal. Others
have walked here, it seems. Yet no fellow travellers share
the cold nocturnal journey. The moon's full eye is round
with surprise, as if no one before has ever been pinned
by its sharp unsettling gaze. Each must pass this way alone
on the only road that winds through the branchy woods,
owl-winged in deepest midnight, somewhere in a country
whose border was crossed without map or guide in a time
lost long ago. Now and then a star gleams down between
leaves, and in its quiet light an aureole of memory swells,
catches in the back of the throat for a moment, then ebbs,
or was possibly blinked away. Occasionally, voices carry
on the night wind, whispers half heard, as if companions
might be near after all. But whichever way the head turns
the breeze shifts, slipping through shadow trees; murmurs
die away, imagined maybe, the gossip of wolves mocking.
Why have so many, treading this exiles' road, left unreadable
signs for those who follow? Why have none come blundering
back through the forest with flapping hands, crying out
Turn around, there is nothing to lead you on, nothing beyond?
Futile surely to stand here in tears on the echo-less road,
while the owl hunts beyond vision and dawn lies sunk
under tangled roots. Answers will not be caught like leaves
for luck in the hand. Better to accept there is no way back,
better to say only, *The mystery leads us on*. For the mystery,
always just out of sight, may perhaps reveal itself in the light
of the open field when the pilgrimage ends on the other side,
and the saints and the trumpets howl.

II.
Across the brown field, a magpie hunches on the topmost branch
of a leafless ash. Gulls float high in the grey sky, remote as jets.
Below, a hare huddles down among clods of earth in frozen plough,
while rooks rise and fall like flies from the fingertips of dim woods.

On the path, a crow lies stark on its back, claws curled, wings spread
in a dull defeat of flight. I skirt around it, my feet on dead leaves
breaking a silence almost too thick to breathe. On such an iron day
I cannot stop to mourn, must keep insistent questions sternly mute.

Instead, let mind uncouple from body, feel comfort in the dumb motion
of blood and bone obeying. Besides, there is contentment in this dense
reflective landscape, misted air refusing a sense of distance, dusk
beginning to fall like snow and numb the stinging hurt of edges.

Nothing is sure any more, not even the hare, the magpie, solitude.
Almost I could believe that somewhere quite close, another figure
is walking the same road. For a moment I imagine that if I caught up
I could slip my arm into his for warmth. We would go on together.

III.
Hard to look back
down the dark
hollow way
and glimpse
at its distant end
only a pinprick
of illusive light,
a star not simply
too far to imagine
but surely already
burned out.

Looking ahead
through thin trees
in December mist
is easier perhaps.
Nothing there
but what might be
a glimmer,
peering forward
for a flickering candle,
a match just lit,
or a will o' the wisp.

IV.
I want to learn
how to speak the language of owl,
so when I'm on the dark road
I can call deep into the trees, knowing
I'm not alone after all, trusting that
my frightened voice will quaver out
in owl-speak and be answered
with a wooing reassurance.

When I hear rabbit shriek in the night,
I want owl to fly low across the ash
and say, "That's just the way of weasels.
That's how it is with we who hunt
in the dark of a trackless forest."
I want to understand how to hide,
how to see in the places of no light.

I want to spread my wings and glide
as owl glides, silent and moon-eyed
in a world so familiar I know to dodge
this tangled ivy, these broken branches,
poaching through sleeping trees
with consummate, feathered ease.

I want to ask, "How is it, owl.
in the shadow of the high pine?
How is it to tear the skin off mice
and read the scents of blindness?
Do you have the wisdom of sorrow?"
But the trees remain deep in quiet.

V.

In the bone light of a quarter moon,
from whose far country snow was falling,
a fox loped out of the wood, low-bellied,
and crossed the road on stealthy feet.

I could see the night dark in his eyes,
his fearful hunger, and the silver of stars
glinting in the guard-hairs along his spine.
Long after he'd gone, his neat chain of prints

scripted a cipher on the snow-lit path.
Beauty to quicken the heart, the breath,
swift vanishing, yet a scent of morning, a hint
of silver leading me on through skeletal trees.

Lunacy

The room is full of shadows that defy sleep,
so in the end I surrender, get out of bed,
and go to watch the greater night beyond
the glass, where a blade of moon, molten
in the star-flung sky, draws the eye
to its remote indifference.

I know better than to seek for answers
among the cloudy constellations hung
to seduce in cryptic tracery,
yet I succumb and like a fool I ask:
if he were four years further into
the chronic enigma of disease,
joints slowly stiffening and sickening,
would he be wishing for the pain to end?
Would he now be grateful that it had?

Words flicker like dreams in the mind,
or satellites, disguised as shooting stars,
that beam intelligence in unbreakable code.

Oh moon, slicing steady and silent across
the spangled dark, I know you can't respond.
I know you are, for all your lofty grace,
no more than dust under astronauts' boots.
But what is there left to do on this cold
midnight except stare out into the space
beyond acceptance, searching galaxies
for predictions of a different past?

Behold

Notice the calligraphy of swans
curving with grace the pliant water.
Above them the rainbow's perfect silk
dips its ends in the golden river.

Consider the brawling of wind,
rooks scattering the rocking air
like fistfuls of questions flung: what
is gravity? What is loveliness?

What is the heron for, the elegant fisher
who lifts my heart on the surprise
of her wings till rain stings my skin
and I touch the rough fur that curls
along the back of clouds?

When I fall it's to the tenderness
of earth. Come close, observe
thin flecks of glimmering chalk
in the granular chew of a molehill
dark on winter grass.
                  Then ask a jay
or a kingfisher, why those feathers
of dazzling blue? Is it for the hawk
the scarlet target of a robin's breast?

More questions, conundrums, corners.
So much hidden, so much promised
in the river's journey, the sky's infinity,
the fold of a leaf. And I'd thought there
was nothing before me, no way of filling
the hours between your death and mine.

Sunday Unexpectedly

This morning there were angels in the tangle of hazel by the river.
I heard the soft burr of their feathers, the flutter and rustle
in the golden flitting of first-born leaves, and I heard them singing
a thread of anthem that might have been Bach or Brahms or birds
inspired by the glory of trees to lift up their hearts to the hills in song,
and the river was full of praise.

This morning the grass in the meadow was dazzled by sparkling stars of
flowers who must have been singing too, for the blue air shone and shook
with its choir of sound, and the glistening buds of chestnut broke free
of winter to listen. And all was sweet in the fragrance of violets;
the sun warmed the birthing of bees in the blossoming cherry, and the
angels sang on in the trembling beaks of wrens. I stood still in the tangle
of hazel, and the river was full of praise.

The Beauty of Morning Speaks

I am all new beginnings. In me
the tender light is rocked. I sing
to the cradle, the wondering child.
I tell of the leaves, their frail emerging,
and of the fern's soft tongue unfurling
to the ardent loveliness of spring.
I am your journey, yours the courage
to take the first step away from grief.
More is possible than you believe.

A Time to Embrace

Love and grief are of the same tree,
as inseparable as twig from bud
or trunk from the consolation of bark.
If love can grow year by year
as rings increase and branches
reach their leaftips closer to God,
then why imagine grief
diminishes as time goes by?

In days of light, the night retreats
then rallies to recapture winter.
The moon wanes before the sun's fist
but fruits again, bright as before.
The oak loses its leaves, stands
stripped in the freezing months
yet fosters within it renewal,
a coming again to birth.

Grief may shed leaves in an icy wind,
but it doesn't wane into some everdark,
or sleep mute beneath the graven earth.
It lodges as a seed in the body—
the heart—to be nurtured there
through numbness into light,
essential for the journey forward,
vital as the love that gave it life.

IRON Press is among the country's longest
established independent literary publishers.
The press began operations in 1973 with IRON
Magazine which ran for 83 editions until 1997.
Since 1975 we have also brought out a regular list
of individual collections of poetry, fiction and
drama plus various anthologies ranging from
*Voices of Conscience, Limerick Nation, The
Poetry of Perestroika, 100 Island Poems* and *Cold
Iron, Ghost Stories from the 21st Century* and
forthcoming, *Trees* (poems) and *Aliens* (fiction).

The press is one of the leading independent
publishers of haiku in the UK.
Since 2013 we have also run a biennial IRON
Press Festival round the harbour in our
native Cullercoats. The IRON OR Festival took
place in June 2019.

We are delighted to be a part of Inpress Ltd, which
was set up by Arts Council England to support
independent literary publishers.
Go to our website (www.ironpress.co.uk)
for full details of our titles and activities.